Do It Yourself
HOMESCHOOL
JOURNALS

Copyright Information

Do It YOURSELF Homeschool journal, and electronic printable downloads are for Home and Family use only. You may make copies of these materials for only the children in your household.

For information on using these materials for businesses, co-ops, summer camps, day camps, daycare, afterschool program, churches, or schools please contact us for licensing.

Contact Us:

The Thinking Tree LLC

617 N. Swope St. Greenfield, IN 46140. United States

317.622.8852 PHONE (Dial +1 outside of the USA) 267.712.7889 FAX

www.DyslexiaGames.com

jbrown@DyslexiaGames.com

Made in the USA
Monee, IL
20 August 2020